ESSENTIAL SONGS FOR

violin

T0039913

Available for
FLUTE, CLARINET, ALTO SAX, TENOR SAX, TRUMPET,
HORN, TROMBONE, VIOLIN, VIOLA, CELLO

ISBN 978-1-4234-5538-7

HAL•LEONARD®
CORPORATION
7777 W. BLUEMOUND RD. P.O. BOX 13819 MILWAUKEE, WI 53213

Visit Hal Leonard Online at
www.halleonard.com

CONTENTS

ALL SHOOK UP

VIOLIN

Words and Music by OTIS BLACKWELL
and ELVIS PRESLEY

ALL THE WAY

from THE JOKER IS WILD

VIOLIN

Words by SAMMY CAHN
Music by JAMES VEN HEUSEN

AND I LOVE HER

VIOLIN

Words and Music by JOHN LENNON
and PAUL McCARTNEY

ANYONE CAN WHISTLE

from ANYONE CAN WHISTLE

Violin

Words and Music by
STEPHEN SONDHEIM

Slowly and tenderly

AUTUMN LEAVES

English lyrics by JOHNNY MERCER
French lyrics by JACQUES PREVERT
Music by JOSEPH KOSMA

VIOLIN

Slowly, with expression

BABY, I LOVE YOUR WAY

VIOLIN

Words and Music by
PETER FRAMPTON

BACK AT ONE

VIOLIN

Words and Music by
BRIAN McKNIGHT

BEAUTIFUL

VIOLIN

Words and Music by
LINDA PERRY

BECAUSE OF YOU

VIOLIN

Words and Music by KELLY CLARKSON,
DAVID HODGES and BEN MOODY

BENNIE AND THE JETS

VIOLIN

Words and Music by ELTON JOHN
and BERNIE TAUPIN

Slow Rock

BLESS THE BROKEN ROAD

VIOLIN

Words and Music by MARCUS HUMMON,
BOBBY BOYD and JEFF HANNA

BORN FREE

from the Columbia Pictures' Release BORN FREE

VIOLIN

Words by DON BLACK
Music by JOHN BARRY

BRING HIM HOME

from LES MISÉRABLES

VIOLIN

Music by CLAUDE-MICHEL SCHÖNBERG
Lyrics by ALAIN BOUBLIL and HERBERT KRETZMER

Moderately slow

BREATHE

VIOLIN

Words and Music by HOLLY LAMAR
and STEPHANIE BENTLEY

Moderately fast

BYE BYE LOVE

VIOLIN

Words and Music by FELICE BRYANT
and BOUDLEAUX BRYANT

CALIFORNIA GIRLS

VIOLIN

Words and Music by BRIAN WILSON
and MIKE LOVE

CAN YOU FEEL THE LOVE TONIGHT

from Walt Disney Pictures' THE LION KING

VIOLIN

Music by ELTON JOHN
Lyrics by TIM RICE

Pop Ballad

THE CHICKEN DANCE

Violin

By TERRY RENDALL
and WERNER THOMAS

CLIMB EV'RY MOUNTAIN

from THE SOUND OF MUSIC

VIOLIN

Lyrics by OSCAR HAMMERSTEIN II
Music by RICHARD RODGERS

Majestically

CRAZY LITTLE THING CALLED LOVE

VIOLIN

Words and Music by
FREDDIE MERCURY

COMPLICATED

VIOLIN

Words and Music by AVRIL LAVIGNE,
LAUREN CHRISTY, SCOTT SPOCK
and GRAHAM EDWARDS

CROCODILE ROCK

VIOLIN

Words and Music by ELTON JOHN
and BERNIE TAUPIN

DANCING QUEEN

VIOLIN

Words and Music by BENNY ANDERSSON,
BJORN ULVAEUS and STIG ANDERSON

Strong Rock

DON'T KNOW WHY

VIOLIN

Words and Music by
JESSE HARRIS

DREAM LOVER

VIOLIN

Words and Music by
BOBBY DARIN

DROPS OF JUPITER
(Tell Me)

VIOLIN

Words and Music by PAT MONAHAN,
JIMMY STAFFORD, ROB HOTCHKISS,
CHARLIE COLIN and SCOTT UNDERWOOD

D.S. al Coda

CODA

DUST IN THE WIND

VIOLIN

Words and Music by
KERRY LIVGREN

EASTER PARADE

from AS THOUSANDS CHEER

VIOLIN

Words and Music by
IRVING BERLIN

ENDLESS LOVE

VIOLIN

Words and Music by
LIONEL RICHIE

FEVER

VIOLIN

Words and Music by JOHN DAVENPORT
and EDDIE COOLEY

FIRE AND RAIN

VIOLIN

Words and Music by
JAMES TAYLOR

THE FIRST CUT IS THE DEEPEST

VIOLIN

Words and Music by
CAT STEVENS

Moderately

THE FOOL ON THE HILL

VIOLIN

Words and Music by JOHN LENNON
and PAUL McCARTNEY

Slowly

FOOTLOOSE
Theme from the Paramount Motion Picture FOOTLOOSE

VIOLIN

Words by DEAN PITCHFORD
and KENNY LOGGINS
Music by KENNY LOGGINS

Fast Rock

FROM A DISTANCE

VIOLIN

Words and Music by
JULIE GOLD

GO AWAY, LITTLE GIRL

VIOLIN

Words and Music by GERRY GOFFIN
and CAROLE KING

GOOD VIBRATIONS

VIOLIN

Words and Music by BRIAN WILSON
and MIKE LOVE

GOT MY MIND SET ON YOU

VIOLIN

Words and Music by
RUDY CLARK

A GROOVY KIND OF LOVE

VIOLIN

Words and Music by TONI WINE
and CAROLE BAYER SAGER

HAPPY TOGETHER

VIOLIN

Words and Music by GARRY BONNER
and ALAN GORDON

HAPPY TRAILS

from the Television Series THE ROY ROGERS SHOW

VIOLIN

Words and Music by
DALE EVANS

HEAVEN

VIOLIN

Words and Music by BRYAN ADAMS
and JIM VALLANCE

HEAVEN

VIOLIN

Words and Music by HENRY GARZA,
JOEY GARZA and RINGO GARZA

HELLO

VIOLIN

Words and Music by
LIONEL RICHIE

Slow Ballad

HIGH HOPES

VIOLIN

Words by SAMMY CAHN
Music by JAMES VAN HEUSEN

HOW CAN YOU MEND A BROKEN HEART

Violin

Words and Music by BARRY GIBB
and ROBIN GIBB

Slow beat

HOW SWEET IT IS (TO BE LOVED BY YOU)

VIOLIN

Words and Music by EDWARD HOLLAND
LAMONT DOZIER and BRIAN HOLLAND

I GOT YOU
(I Feel Good)

VIOLIN

Words and Music by
JAMES BROWN

(Spoken:) Hey!

I HOPE YOU DANCE

VIOLIN

Words and Music by TIA SILLERS
and MARK D. SANDERS

I JUST CALLED TO SAY I LOVE YOU

VIOLIN

Words and Music by
STEVIE WONDER

Moderately

I LEFT MY HEART IN SAN FRANCISCO

VIOLIN

Words by DOUGLASS CROSS
Music by GEORGE CORY

Moderately

I SHOT THE SHERIFF

VIOLIN

Words and Music by
BOB MARLEY

Moderately slow, with a beat

I WANT TO HOLD YOUR HAND

VIOLIN

Words and Music by JOHN LENNON
PAUL McCARTNEY

Moderately, with a beat

I'LL BE THERE

VIOLIN

Words and Music by BERRY GORDY,
HAL DAVIS, WILLIE HUTCH
and BOB WEST

Moderately

I'LL BE

VIOLIN

Words and Music by
EDWIN McCAIN

63

I'M WITH YOU

VIOLIN

Words and Music by AVRIL LAVIGNE, LAUREN CHRISTY,
SCOTT SPOCK and GRAHAM EDWARDS

IF

VIOLIN

Words and Music by
DAVID GATES

IF I HAD A HAMMER
(The Hammer Song)

Words and Music by LEE HAYS
and PETE SEEGER

THE IMPRESSION THAT I GET

VIOLIN

Words and Music by DICKY BARRETT
and JOE GITTLEMAN

IN THE MOOD

VIOLIN

By JOE GARLAND

IT'S A SMALL WORLD

from "it's a small world" at Disneyland Park and Magic Kingdom Park

VIOLIN

Words and Music by RICHARD M. SHERMAN
and ROBERT B. SHERMAN

IT'S TOO LATE

VIOLIN

Words and Music by CAROLE KING
and TONI STERN

Slowly

ITSY BITSY TEENIE WEENIE
YELLOW POLKADOT BIKINI

VIOLIN

Words and Music by PAUL VANCE
and LEE POCKRISS

Moderately

THEME FROM "JURASSIC PARK"

from the Universal Motion Picture JURASSIC PARK

VIOLIN

Composed by
JOHN WILLIAMS

KING OF THE ROAD

VIOLIN

Words and Music by
ROGER MILLER

LA BAMBA

VIOLIN

By RITCHIE VALENS

Moderate Latin Rock

To Coda

D.S. al Coda

CODA

LET IT BE

VIOLIN

Words and Music by JOHN LENNON
PAUL McCARTNEY

77

LISTEN TO WHAT THE MAN SAID

VIOLIN

Words and Music by
PAUL and LINDA McCARTNEY

THE LOCO-MOTION

VIOLIN

Words and Music by GERRY GOFFIN
and CAROLE KING

Moderately

LOUIE, LOUIE

VIOLIN

Words and Music by
RICHARD BERRY

LOVE ME TENDER

VIOLIN

Words and Music by ELVIS PRESLEY
and VERA MATSON

LUCY IN THE SKY WITH DIAMONDS

VIOLIN

Words and Music by JOHN LENNON
and PAUL McCARTNEY

MAMBO NO. 5
(A Little Bit Of...)

VIOLIN

Original Music by DAMASO PEREZ PRADO
Words by LOU BEGA and ZIPPY

ME AND BOBBY McGEE

VIOLIN

Words and Music by KRIS KRISTOFFERSON
and FRED FOSTER

A MOMENT LIKE THIS

VIOLIN

Words and Music by JOHN REID
and JORGEN KJELL ELOFSSON

Moderately slow

MY FAVORITE THINGS

from THE SOUND OF MUSIC

VIOLIN

Lyrics by OSCAR HAMMERSTEIN II
Music by RICHARD RODGERS

Lively, with spirit

THE ODD COUPLE

Theme from the Paramount Picture THE ODD COUPLE
Theme from the Paramount Television Series THE ODD COUPLE

VIOLIN

By NEAL HEFTI

ON TOP OF SPAGHETTI

VIOLIN

Words and Music by
TOM GLAZER

Moderately fast, with spirit

100 YEARS

VIOLIN

Words and Music by
JOHN ONDRASIK

ONE NOTE SAMBA
(Samba de uma nota so)

VIOLIN

Original Lyrics by NEWTON MENDONCA
English Lyrics by ANTONIO CARLOS JOBIM
Music by ANTONIO CARLOS JOBIM

PETER COTTONTAIL

VIOLIN

Words and Music by STEVE NELSON
and JACK ROLLINS

PUPPY LOVE

VIOLIN

Words and Music by
PAUL ANKA

Moderately slow

QUE SERA, SERA
(Whatever Will Be, Will Be)
from THE MAN WHO KNEW TOO MUCH

Violin

Words and Music by JAY LIVINGSTON
and RAY EVANS

R.O.C.K. IN THE U.S.A
(A Salute to 60's Rock)

VIOLIN

Words and Music by
JOHN MELLENCAMP

Fast Rock

THE RAINBOW CONNECTION
from THE MUPPET MOVIE

VIOLIN

Words and Music by PAUL WILLIAMS
and KENNETH L. ASCHER

RAINDROPS KEEP FALLIN' ON MY HEAD

from BUTCH CASSIDY AND THE SUNDANCE KID

VIOLIN

Lyric by HAL DAVID
Music by BURT BACHARACH

ROCKIN' ROBIN

VIOLIN

Words and Music by
J. THOMAS

SAILING

VIOLIN

Words and Music by
CHRISTOPHER CROSS

SEE YOU LATER, ALLIGATOR

VIOLIN

Words and Music by
ROBERT GUIDR...

SEVENTY SIX TROMBONES
from Meredith Willson's THE MUSIC MAN

By MEREDITH WILLSON

VIOLIN

March tempo

SHAKE, RATTLE AND ROLL

VIOLIN

Words and Music by
CHARLES CALHOUN

SHOUT

VIOLIN

Words and Music by ROLAND ORZABAL
and IAN STANLEY

SIXTEEN GOING ON SEVENTEEN
from THE SOUND OF MUSIC

VIOLIN

Lyrics by OSCAR HAMMERSTEIN II
Music by RICHARD RODGERS

SMOOTH

VIOLIN

Words by ROB THOMAS
Music by ROB THOMAS and ITALL SHUR

Medium Latin Rock

SO NICE
(Summer Samba)

VIOLIN

Original Words and Music by MARCOS VALLE
and PAULO SERGIO VALLE
English Words by NORMAN GIMBEL

Moderately

THE SOUND OF MUSIC

from THE SOUND OF MUSIC

Violin

Lyrics by OSCAR HAMMERSTEIN II
Music by RICHARD RODGERS

With much expression

SPINNING WHEEL

VIOLIN

Words and Music by
DAVID CLAYTON THOMAS

Funky, moderate Rock

SPLISH SPLASH

VIOLIN

Words and Music by BOBBY DARIN
and MURRAY KAUFMAN

STAND BY ME

VIOLIN

Words and Music by JERRY LEIBER,
MIKE STOLLER and BEN E. KING

Sunny

VIOLIN

Words and Music by
BOBBY HEBB

Moderate Rock

SUPERCALIFRAGILISTICEXPIALIDOCIOUS

from Walt Disney's MARY POPPINS

VIOLIN

Words and Music by RICHARD M. SHERMAN
and ROBERT B. SHERMAN

SURFIN' U.S.A.

VIOLIN

Words and Music by
CHUCK BERRY

Solid Shuffle beat

TAKIN' CARE OF BUSINESS

VIOLIN

Words and Music by
RANDY BACHMAN

TEARS IN HEAVEN

VIOLIN

Words and Music by ERIC CLAPTON
and WILL JENNINGS

TENNESSEE WALTZ

VIOLIN

Words and Music by REDD STEWART
and PEE WEE KING

THAT'LL BE THE DAY

Violin

Words and Music by JERRY ALLISON,
NORMAN PETTY and BUDDY HOLLY

THIS LOVE

VIOLIN

Words and Music by ADAM LEVIN
and JESSE CARMICHAEL

Moderate Rock

TIE A YELLOW RIBBON
ROUND THE OLE OAK TREE

Violin

Words and Music by L. RUSSELL BROWN
and IRWIN LEVINE

TIJUANA TAXI

VIOLIN

Words by JOHNNY FLAMINGO
Music by ERVAN "BUD" COLEMAN

Moderately

TRUE COLORS

VIOLIN

Words and Music by BILLY STEINBERG
and TOM KELLY

THE TWIST

VIOLIN

Words and Music by
HANK BALLARD

UP WHERE WE BELONG

from the Paramount Picture AN OFFICER AND A GENTLEMAN

VIOLIN

Words by WILL JENNINGS
Music by BUFFY SAINTE-MARIE and JACK NITZSCHE

WALKING IN MEMPHIS

VIOLIN

Words and Music by
MARC COHN

D.S. al Coda 1

CODA 1

Suddenly slowly, freely

Tempo I

2

D.C. al Coda 2

CODA 2

THE WAY YOU LOOK TONIGHT
from SWING TIME

Violin

Words by DOROTHY FIELDS
Music by JEROME KERN

WE ARE FAMILY

VIOLIN

Words and Music by NILE RODGERS
and BERNARD EDWARDS

WE ARE THE CHAMPIONS

VIOLIN

Words and Music by
FREDDIE MERCURY

WE BUILT THIS CITY

Violin

Words and Music by BERNIE TAUPIN, MARTIN PAGE,
DENNIS LAMBERT and PETER WOLF

WE'VE ONLY JUST BEGUN

VIOLIN

Words and Music by ROGER NICHOLS
and PAUL WILLIAMS

WHITE FLAG

Violin

Words and Music by RICK NOWELS,
ROLLO ARMSTRONG and DIDO ARMSTRONG

Moderately slow

A WHOLE NEW WORLD

from Walt Disney's ALADDIN

Violin

Music by ALAN MENKEN
Lyrics by TIM RICE

Y.M.C.A.

VIOLIN

Words and Music by JACQUES MORALI
HENRI BELOLO and VICTOR WILLIS

Yesterday

VIOLIN

Words and Music by JOHN LENNON
and PAUL McCARTNEY

Moderately, with expression

YOU ARE MY SUNSHINE

VIOLIN

Words and Music by
JIMMIE DAVIS

Lively

YOU LIGHT UP MY LIFE

VIOLIN

Words and Music by
JOSEPH BROOKS

YOU ARE THE MUSIC IN ME

VIOLIN

from the Disney Channel Original Movie HIGH SCHOOL MUSICAL 2

Words and Music by
JAMIE HOUSTON

Moderately fast Rock

139

YOU'RE BEAUTIFUL

Violin

Words and Music by JAMES BLUNT,
SACHA SKARBEK and AMANDA GHOST

Moderately slow

YOU'RE STILL THE ONE

Violin

Words and Music by SHANIA TWAIN
and ROBERT JOHN LANGE

YOU'VE GOT A FRIEND IN ME

from Walt Disney's TOY STORY

VIOLIN

Music and Lyrics by
RANDY NEWMAN

YOUR SONG

VIOLIN

Words and Music by ELTON JOHN
and BERNIE TAUPIN

ZOOT SUIT RIOT

VIOLIN

Words and Music by
STEVE PERRY

Spoken: *Blow, dad-dy!*